# ROAD WARRIOR'S COMPANION:
# PRAYER VOL. 1

# ROAD WARRIOR'S COMPANION: PRAYER VOL. 1

Daniel de Eagle

Edited by Tammy Hensel
Designed by Marcus C Stallworth

ISBN: 0692409750
ISBN 13: 9780692409756
Library of Congress Control Number: 2015904837
Daniel de Eagle, Euless, TX

# Dedication

In honor of the memory of my father in the Lord of blessed memory Dr. Tayo Adeyemi aka Pastor Trailblazer. It was said of him by men of renown in our time that they couldn't wait to see the fruits that will spring forth from his going home to glory in the way of the seed. As a grain of wheat he fell into the earth and died. I stand to testify that I am one of the many fruits of the unsung hero Dr. Tayo who walked amongst us. We are still discovering his worth. I also dedicate these reflective thoughts to my childhood prayer partner and wife of 18 years Nikki. To my 3Ps who also double as my politician, prophet and psalmist Daddy loves you loads. Thanks for letting me slip into my man cave to be a blessing to others.

# Foreword

I have known Daniel de Eagle since his days as a student in a Bible college in London, England. Now living in the United States, Brother Daniel has continued to grow in his study and practice of prayer. This book is not written by a novice or a researcher. It is written by a man who has personally experienced the power of prayer and continues to walk through its disciplines.

Acts 17 relates the ministry of the apostle Paul in Thessalonica. The text tells us that he ministered in the local synagogue for three Sabbaths. In other words, in three weeks Paul established a Christian community based on the foundations of Christian doctrine and lifestyle. In three weeks of Spirit-anointed ministry much can occur!

Daniel de Eagle gives us a month of Spirit-anointed ministry in this book. I encourage you to take this month-long journey and allow the Holy Spirit to "turn your world upside down."

Dr. Doug Beacham
>   General Superintendent and Presiding Bishop
>   The International Pentecostal Holiness Church
>   Oklahoma City, Oklahoma, USA

Other Endorsements:
It is said that prayer is better caught than taught and I have learnt over the years that the best way to learn how to pray is to

spend time in prayer with people who know how to pray. Daniel de Eagle is one individual that I know who knows how to pray. You may not have the luxury of being in the same prayer room with him, but you can allow the nuggets contained in "Road Warrior's Companion" to fuel your passion for prayer. I highly recommend this book on prayer.

Tony Oliha
Senior Minister, New Wine Church

We must never underestimate the importance and power of prayer. Prayer bridges the gap in communication between God and man. With this said, Daniel de Eagle has created a valuable tool that is a bridge towards us and heaven. His prayer manual is a step by step, day by day tool to help us cultivate an effective and consistent prayer life. I have no doubt that this book will challenge you to stir up the gift within and take your prayer life to the next level. Thank you, sir, for taking the time to bless us with such a gift!

Kunlé Oyedeji
Pastor: The Cornerstone Church, UK

I have watched Daniel de Eagle's life closely for a number of years. He is a man who believes in prayer, loves to pray and shares this passion with others. Let the words and strategies set forth in this devotional deepen your friendship with God and start, re-start, or propel forward the transformation process of your heart. A life guided by prayer can have a profound impact on the world--go for it!

Joseph Borsh
Lead Chaplain, Hope Workplace Chaplains, Inc.

Prayer is the language of faith. It is the arena where the future is determined. This little book has big implications for those who determine to win invisible battles. The truths are timeless, the lessons are price-less and the rewards are boundless.

Frank Ofosu-Appiah

Founder and Senior Pastor of All Nations Church.

General Overseer of the Living Springs International Churches.

# About The Author

Daniel de Eagle is a servant leader, prayer missionary from the Generation X timeline. He serves as the Lead Prayer Strategist and Trainer at When Eagles Pray Trainer (W.E.P.T.) Inc., a strategic online and in-person prayer resourcing service to the local and global Body of Christ. Known for his strong flow in prophetic intercession and deep yet simplistic teaching insight on everything about prayer for all levels of Christian maturity, Daniel has been actively involved in the prayer ministry for 29 years. He lives by the prayer mantra that "Prayer is from the heart and about results," based on James 5:16. He has served on the leadership team of various church-led and ancillary ministry-led prayer initiatives across the continents of Europe, Africa and North America. He currently serves on the socio-media team for the National Day of Prayer & Worship, UK. Daniel has a strong passion for marriage and the family, prayer and the marketplace. Daniel completed his Diploma in Christian Ministries program with emphasis on Youth and Community development at CICM, UK, in 1997. Daniel has been married to his wife and ministry partner, Nikki, for 18 years. They have three children. They cohost the yearly Marriage Reignited Gala event for married heterosexual couples. Follow Daniel on Twitter @prayaminute | Instagram: daniel_de_eagle | YouTube Channel: Daniel de Eagle

For the present day or techie generations the following quote better captures who Daniel is:

I'm not esoteric but I spit lyrics with a historic, dynamic, economic, romantic and prophetic undertone as a timeless psychedelic cleric on a Word hallucinogenic with a unique homiletic. My trailblazing mentor the late Dr. Tayo Adeyemi christened me Bayustic Acclamatura.

~Daniel de Eagle

# Part One
# Need/Dependence

Prayer begins as a desire, evolves to a discipline, and grows into a delight. The cycle then restarts.

**OBSERVATIONS:**

Those of us on the prayer journey first experience prayer as a desire based on seeing someone else pray or just having a deep longing to pray. This early prayer stage may not be fun, but the more we do it the more we enjoy it.

It is important to be observant of your prayer life with a view to gaining experience and growing. Hunger is the restart button for the prayer life cyclical progression. You are not at the same level the second, third or fourth time around the learning curve when you pray. As you hunger for more understanding in prayer you will keep maturing.

Read Psalm 37:4 and Philippians 3:12-14.

**RECORD YOUR OWN OBSERVATIONS.**

_____
_____
_____
_____
_____
_____

True prayer requires dependence on God. We may claim to pray, but then often there is no trace of real dependence reflecting in what we say while praying. Go figure.

## OBSERVATIONS:

Many people pray, but to whom or what? From a neutral observer's standpoint, the content of our prayers, if indeed they are to God, should have traces of our need for God's intervention and our dependence on Him. The first account in Genesis of humans praying focused on dependence, not need. Petitions for needs occurred over time. Let us keep to the original trend—dependence first, needs next.

Read James 2:23 and Genesis 4:26.

## RECORD YOUR OWN OBSERVATIONS.

_____

_____

_____

_____

_____

_____

_____

_____

# Day Three

Prayer is ultimately about reconnecting with "The Source." Don't be unplugged and powerless. Start getting connected or reconnected.

## OBSERVATIONS:

Mankind first began to pray after sin disconnected us from the presence of God. The goal when it comes to prayer is to be in the presence of God. Getting back into permanent relationship with God begins with prayer through the acts of repentance, confession, receiving of forgiveness and acceptance of the Lordship of Jesus. No longer is there shame when praying to God. The prayer connection with God of those not submitted to His Lordship is temporary, based solely on God's merciful love. Remember God is Love and He is God of all whether we accept Him or not. He shows mercy through prayer to whoever He wills.

Read 1 John 1:5-10 and John 3:16-18

## RECORD YOUR OWN OBSERVATIONS.

_____

_____

_____

_____

_____

# Day Four

When praying, we love it when our heart palpitates with antici-pation at the prospect of an encounter with God. It only goes to show we need Him.

## OBSERVATIONS:

Watch the unfolding of a new romance. He sees the beautiful lady for the first time. His heart palpitates. Despite the butterflies, he says "hi." Her response brings heaven to earth. Excitement fills the air!

We can have the same thrill every time we engage the Holy Spirit in prayer. Our bond with Him deepens as we spend quality time in prayer, in the Word, and in worship. That can be very exciting! We learn to talk with Him daily—during our morning jog, while driving to work, and throughout our myriad of daily activities. This keeps our love relationship with Him as fresh and exciting as any romance.

Read Psalm 42:1;  John 3: 3-5; Romans 8:26 and John 14:26.

## RECORD YOUR OWN OBSERVATIONS.

_____

_____

_____

_____

_____

_____

## Day Five

When it comes to prayer we're clueless while the Holy Spirit is all clued-up. Keep depending on God.

OBSERVATIONS:

Many times we think we know what to pray. We assume it's a matter of opening our mouths and asking for what we want. Hold on a minute soldier. There's someone else involved in the prayer deal called the Holy Spirit. After the physical departure of Lord Jesus from this world, the Holy Spirit, who came on the day of Pentecost, began to teach us how we ought to pray. Let's not rush into prayer next time. Let's ask the Holy Spirit to teach us to pray as we should be praying.

Read Romans 8:26.

RECORD YOUR OWN OBSERVATIONS.

_____
_____
_____
_____
_____
_____
_____
_____
_____

# Day Six

The root focus of prayer from God's perspective is for you and me to depend on Him every time we pray and not so much for us to get answers.

## OBSERVATIONS:

When we pray, we are so much concerned about getting answers to our prayers from God, like our kids are about us meeting their needs. As parents the deep cry of our hearts is for our kids to hang out with us. Yes we do want to meet their needs, but more than needs we want them to be with us. Our Father in heaven in the same manner has the agenda that we hang out with him. If us asking him for things is part of what it will take, then so be it, but He has greater things in mind than meeting our needs if we go the extra mile and spend time with Him.

Read Exodus 20:4-5; and John 21:15-16.

## RECORD YOUR OWN OBSERVATIONS.

_____

_____

_____

_____

_____

_____

# Part Two
# Prayer Attitude/Methods/
# Time Management

# Day Seven

A prayer scope based on looking downwards and around is limited, but a prayer scope fixed above lets you soar like an eagle and remain balanced.

## OBSERVATIONS:

When we look down our vision is limited, but when looking up we tend to see more. We all have challenges in life, but it is within our prerogative how we see our challenges. How much better to pray looking up to get God's perspective rather than looking down in our human understanding where discouragement can easily overcome us.

Read Psalm 121:1-2 and Isaiah 40:31.

## RECORD YOUR OWN OBSERVATIONS.

_____
_____
_____
_____
_____
_____
_____
_____
_____
_____

# Day Eight

Harmonizing my prayer perspective with God's perspective through His Word has an extraordinary way of ensuring effectiveness in praying.

## OBSERVATIONS:

If you are about to go through the unknown it could be very scary, but if you know someone who passed through your unknown a timeless number of times, then it makes sense to seek his or her perspective on the matter. There is no prayer scenario that we face that God does not have a perspective on or understand. It's wise to seek his perspective through His Word when we pray.

Read 1 John 5:14.

## RECORD YOUR OWN OBSERVATIONS.

_____

_____

_____

_____

_____

_____

_____

_____

_____

# Day Nine

When we pray from a longing heart for God guided by His word, our prayers hit the target. When we pray selfishly, we pray amiss.

## OBSERVATIONS:

The degree to which we effectively wield the force of prayer is proportional to how much we hunger and thirst after God's Word. Knowing God's Word helps us better communicate with Him. Prayer should stem from a love for God reflected in a consummate desire for knowing and doing God's word.

Read 1 John 5:14; 2 Chronicles 26:5; and Psalm 42:1.

## RECORD YOUR OWN OBSERVATIONS.

_____

_____

_____

_____

_____

_____

_____

_____

_____

_____

Praying haphazardly isn't okay. We should never allow the circumference of our prayers be determined by external factors.

OBSERVATIONS:
As a child in school, I studied a topic called circle theorem. We students dreaded it, and those who grasped it were regarded as the geeks. Everything in circle theorem revolved around the center. Any calculation we did without figuring it in came out wrong. God is the center of any prayer circle. So long as we keep letting Him be center when we are praying we'll be okay. When we allow external factors like fear, doubt, or even the troubling situation that is bothering us to take over the center slot, then the prayer outcome is not good.

Read Genesis 13:14; Deuteronomy 6:5; James 1:6-7; 1 Cor. 6:19-20; and Matthew 21:13.

RECORD YOUR OWN OBSERVATIONS.

_____
_____
_____
_____
_____
_____
_____

# Day Eleven

A maximized prayer time entails allowing your whole being to cooperate with the physical promptings of the Holy Spirit.

## OBSERVATIONS:

When the Holy Spirit invites you to pray, He invites all of you. Prayer is a total spirit, soul and body experience. To leave or deny any part from the experience is to not love with your all. To pray with our all entails allowing the expressions resulting from praying with the mind and the spirit to be released. When you are sad, tears may flow from your person while praying. When you are happy, it is no coincidence that you are likely to raise your hands in thanks and praise to the Lord. Let us not be ashamed to fall on our knees or lie prostrate before God as we seek to maximize a time of prayer.

Read Matthew 22:37-38; 1 Kings 8:54; Nehemiah 8:6; 1Tim. 2:8; Psalm 141:2; and 1 Corinthians 14:15.

## RECORD YOUR OWN OBSERVATIONS.

_____
_____
_____
_____
_____
_____

# Day Twelve

Praying yourself into God's manifest presence while intentionally staying focused prepares you for precise prayers that yield results.

## OBSERVATIONS:
Those who can maintain focus for an extended period of time tend to get the job done. Results elude us when we pray all over the place instead of focusing on the real need in our hearts. As children, parents and teachers told us to remain focused. Now, the Holy Spirit gently reminds us to stay focused in prayer.

Read Luke 9:28-29; Daniel 9:20-21; and Matthew 26:41.

## RECORD YOUR OWN OBSERVATIONS.

_____

_____

_____

_____

_____

_____

_____

_____

_____

_____

# Day Thirteen

The place of prayer is not a physical location, although a physical location can help you quickly get into the manifest presence of the Lord.

## OBSERVATIONS:

The premise of prayer is faith in an unseen Creator God whose handiwork we see in nature. We tend, as praying individuals, to find a favorite spot inside or outside our homes where nature can help us deepen our communication or connection with God. As a shepherd, David spent most of his time on the mountain sides where he led his sheep to graze. It is understandable that he connected with God most times in this location since he was alone most of the time. Where we feel most alone to express ourselves is an indication of the physical location that connects us with the presence of God. In the presence of God is the place of prayer.

Read John 4:23; Luke 6:12; and Psalm 19.

## RECORD YOUR OWN OBSERVATIONS.

_____

_____

_____

_____

_____

# Day Fourteen

Discipline cultivates quiet, heart-intense prayers. This art is particularly relevant to all growing and driven individuals.

## OBSERVATIONS:

Sometimes at night or during the day you have a strong premonition to pray or you experience anguish or distress. You may or may not know what it is about. You don't have to disturb or wake everyone up with noise because you feel you have to pray loudly. You just need to learn to travail quietly, but with heart intensity to God.

Read Psalm 118:5; Romans 8:26; and Nehemiah 2:4-5.

## RECORD YOUR OWN OBSERVATIONS.

_____

_____

_____

_____

_____

_____

_____

_____

_____

_____

_____

# Day Fifteen

Heaven responds to putting a premium on prayer time.

What you count as valuable becomes valuable to you, even when it is not to others. Heaven has made prayer a valuable commodity. We see this in the life of Jesus and in his teachings while here on earth. Heaven consistently responded in a positive way to Jesus the man based on His putting a premium on prayer. Any individual in biblical times till present day who put a premium on prayer had significant results in their lives. Anyone, no matter who you are, can pray powerful result-oriented prayers if you decide to put a premium on prayer just as heaven does.

Read Luke 18:1 and 1 Samuel 12:23

RECORD YOUR OWN OBSERVATIONS.

_____
_____
_____
_____
_____
_____
_____

# Day Sixteen

When we say we cannot pray like the Old Testament prophet Daniel, we forget that growth occurs in stages.

Daniel prayed three times a day. Often we find it difficult to pray once a day. This does not mean that we should write ourselves off, thinking that we cannot pray like a Daniel. We take baby steps such as: "Father, thank you that I'm alive today. Be with me through my day and help me to be helpful to others. Amen." The number of our words doesn't matter, but rather that our hearts and minds long to talk to the Father of all creation in prayer. The more we take little prayer steps the more our prayer ability and confidence increases.

Read Daniel 6:10-11.

RECORD YOUR OWN OBSERVATIONS.

_____
_____
_____
_____
_____
_____
_____
_____

# Day Seventeen

A high-powered rifle or any gun will ensure damage, even with a silencer. Whether you pray loudly or quietly, what matters is the heart intensity.

## OBSERVATIONS:

People express themselves in diverse manners while praying. It's easy to get caught up in the drama of thinking we have a monopoly on God answering us simply because we only pray in one style. Don't get hung up on the style or method, but let your heart be in your prayers.

Read John 11:42-43 and Matthew 8:13.

## RECORD YOUR OWN OBSERVATIONS.

_____

_____

_____

_____

_____

_____

_____

_____

_____

_____

_____

# Day Eighteen

When praying for big personal life events, think in bite-size. You can easily muster the faith to face it in small chunks.

## OBSERVATIONS:

The size of a life event can be overwhelming. Events like the sudden diagnosis of cancer, death of a loved one, or loss of a job can devastate us. It's important that we do not assume that we can overcome it all at once or alone. That leads to discouragement. Wisdom demands that we divide the task and then focus our prayer energy on the part we face daily, no matter how long it takes. As we see results or get victory in one area of the situation, then we can go on to other aspects of the situation.

Read Luke 16:10 and Isaiah 62:6-7.

## RECORD YOUR OWN OBSERVATIONS.

_____
_____
_____
_____
_____
_____
_____
_____

# Day Nineteen

O ne wields influence through prayer because one makes the most of the time one has.

The more responsibility we get in our jobs and other commitments the more our time becomes a contested commodity. Beware the trap of becoming too busy to pray. All individuals must choose to prioritize prayer time to reap its benefits. Anyone who is willing to pay the time price tag can become a powerful prayer warrior.

Read Ephesians 5:16; Psalm 63:1; and Isaiah 55:6.

RECORD YOUR OWN OBSERVATIONS.

_____

_____

_____

_____

_____

_____

_____

_____

_____

_____

# Day Twenty

Pray ahead of time to keep from straying in time. When you pray early, you get to hear clearly, and you don't pay dearly.

The preparation we make influences the outcomes of the challenges we face. If we rise early we can beat the rush hour traffic on the road and achieve more in our day. Based on the same premise, the choice to pray ahead of critical decisions or hurdles we might face goes a long way in ensuring we make the right decision or avoid possible danger. Prayerful preparation is critical to surviving and ultimately thriving in life.

Read Psalm 63:1 and Matthew 26:41.

RECORD YOUR OWN OBSERVATIONS.

_____
_____
_____
_____
_____
_____
_____
_____
_____

# Day Twenty-one

Wisdom requires that we pray proactively and not reactively. Consistently praying reactively brings into question our spiritual growth.

## OBSERVATIONS:

Everyone, irrespective of faith level and social or economic status, faces problems and challenges in this world. What we do or fail to do ahead of time determines whether we are in panic mode during such challenges or rather have our wits about us to weather the storm and grow from the experience. We can pray proactively for God's protection and provision before we need it, or wait and react by praying in desperation. Jesus charges Peter to pray proactively so that when temptation comes he will not be a victim of panic reaction.

Read Matthew 26:41 and Matthew 25:9-13.

## RECORD YOUR OWN OBSERVATIONS.

_____
_____
_____
_____
_____
_____
_____

# Day Twenty-two

Prayer is valuable and measurable. Subjecting prayer to measurement removes ambiguity in our expectation and enhances its value.

All life, or the living of life, involves measurement. For some reason we generally don't measure prayers or the attendant results. Imagine how much more reassuring our belief system and our prayer life will be if we dare to measure prayer results. Serious prayer measurement requires a journal to list verifiable requests made according to God's Will as shown in His Word. God remains accountable to His Word. We are accountable to diligently and consistently pray with expectation until the answer happens. Then we check it off, intentionally offering thanksgiving to our Father in Heaven.

Read 1 Kings 18:43-44; Luke 22:42-43; James 5:16; and Habakkuk 2:2.

RECORD YOUR OWN OBSERVATIONS.

_____

_____

_____

_____

_____

# Day Twenty-three

In an extended time of prayer, it is advisable to pace yourself and even have an outlined prayer point listing. The flow is not broken.

## OBSERVATIONS:

It's easy to get bored and fall asleep on a long distance train ride, but if you have an engaging novel on hand you find yourself intrigued in your reading for the entire journey. The secret is to be engaged in what you're doing. In an all-night prayer vigil the right preparation, together with a prayer-outlined game plan for the night, will keep you engaged.

Read Luke 6:12-13.

## RECORD YOUR OWN OBSERVATIONS.

_____

_____

_____

_____

_____

_____

_____

_____

_____

# Part Three
# Prayer Content

# Day Twenty-four

Prayer is not rocket science, but there is an art form to the madness. All prayers revolve around engagements with our Heavenly Father, satanic forces, ourselves, and our environment.

OBSERVATIONS:
When we direct prayer to "Our Father in Heaven," we recognize his sovereignty in our lives. The name and the blood of Jesus provide a powerful weapon when spoken against satanic forces that attempt to hinder our prayers. As individuals we gain strength through prayers aimed to encourage ourselves and others. Addressing our environment through prayer occurs when we ask for supernatural intervention in our lives, like Joshua when he prayed and the sun and moon stood still.

Read Luke 11:1-2; Psalm 43:5; Joshua 10:12; Mark 11:12-14, 20-25; 1 Samuel 30:6; Ephesians 6:10-17; and Acts 19:10-12.

RECORD YOUR OWN OBSERVATIONS.

_____
_____
_____
_____
_____
_____

# Day Twenty-five

Seasons of thanksgiving and year round thankful prayers help in releasing our prayer burdens to the Lord when we feel heavy hearted.

## OBSERVATIONS:

The various temperaments we show when praying directly relate to the nature of the issue about which we pray. When we feel overwhelmed we can change the prayer atmosphere by thanking God despite the pain we face. God truly is a burden carrier who wants to bless us. Just as our earthly parents tend to give us more when we show thankfulness, so even more our Heavenly Father rewards a grateful heart.

Read Philippians 4:6 and Luke 17:11-19.

## RECORD YOUR OWN OBSERVATIONS.

_____
_____
_____
_____
_____
_____
_____
_____

# Day Twenty-six

Christians gathering to worship and pray enhance Heaven and Earth's courtship, while Jesus gets the Lordship.

OBSERVATIONS:
When we gather together with thankful hearts focused on Jesus we invite angelic beings to join in the celebration. Each time we praise God, we reenact the jubilation the angels modeled when they announced the good news to the shepherds more than 2000 years ago. In an atmosphere where people bend their knees in worship, the Lordship of Jesus is further reinforced. When collectively our eyes are on Jesus to lift him up with our words and actions, it becomes evident that He is Lord.

Read Psalm 148; John 12:32; and Hebrews 10:25.

RECORD YOUR OWN OBSERVATIONS.

_____
_____
_____
_____
_____
_____
_____
_____

## Day Twenty-seven

P rayer is universal. Exposure to our global siblings praying to the Father helps broaden our prayer understanding. Take time to hear others.

OBSERVATIONS:
Roadrunners think they have an exclusivity to speed until they encounter the high speed train. We better appreciate a life of prayer when we meet people from around the world who pray. You do not necessarily have to physically travel to another place to experience this diversity. Join an international online prayer teleconference to get the feel for this.

Read Acts 2:4 and Ephesians 3:6.

RECORD YOUR OWN OBSERVATIONS.

_____

_____

_____

_____

_____

_____

_____

_____

_____

# Day Twenty-eight

Intercede for government leaders that they may promote policies for peaceful daily living.

## OBSERVATIONS:

Note that the goal of praying for government leaders is not for the souls of these individuals to come to Christ. Rather it is for God to influence the decision making process of those who control the government that the daily peaceful livelihood of the Christian community is not threatened.

Read 1 Timothy 2:1-3 and Romans 13:1-7.

## RECORD YOUR OWN OBSERVATIONS.

_____

_____

_____

_____

_____

_____

_____

_____

_____

_____

_____

# Part Four
# Results

# Day Twenty-nine

God answering our prayers is not a sign that we prayed an effective prayer or that we are living godly lives.

OBSERVATIONS:

It's exciting to have prayers answered. However, the true test of living in obedience is not measured in the number of answered prayers. It comes in discerning what God says through His Word, then praying, and above all living what we discern. The children of Israel cried for meat in the wilderness. God answered their prayer, but also sent a killer plague to punish their whining hearts. It's important we check our motives whenever we pray. Remember, answered prayers are one part of our lives. Let's think obedience to God's Word as we think eternal rewards.

Read Matthew 7:21-23 and Numbers 11:11-13, 18-20, 33.

RECORD YOUR OWN OBSERVATIONS.

_____

_____

_____

_____

_____

_____

_____

# Day Thirty

The greatest prayer legacy parents can give to our children is to pray that they become greater than us in their generation.

## OBSERVATIONS:

Subsequent generations always have greater challenges than their parents. We as parents need to model a prayer routine and help our children set one so that they will be successful adults who achieve greater benefits for humanity. Devotion for a young child can be a 5-second prayer affair: "Good morning, Father in Heaven. Help me today. Amen." That's fine. At other times we ask them to repeat a prayer after us. Be brief. As they grow older we talk and then pray together on issues that concern older children.

Read 1 Kings 1:37.

## RECORD YOUR OWN OBSERVATIONS.

_____

_____

_____

_____

_____

_____

_____

_____

# Road Warrior's Companion: Prayer Vol.1

## I. NEED/DEPENDENCE

Day One – Prayer begins as a desire, evolves to a discipline, and grows into a delight. The cycle then restarts.

Day Two – True prayer requires dependence on God. We may claim to pray, but then there is no trace of real dependence reflecting in what we say while praying. Go figure.

Day Three – Prayer is ultimately about reconnecting with "The Source." Don't be unplugged and powerless. Start getting connected or reconnected.

Day Four –When praying, we love it when our heart palpitates with anticipation at the prospect of an encounter with God. It only goes to show we need Him.

Day Five –When it comes to prayer, we're clueless while the Holy Spirit is all clued-up. Keep depending on God.

Day Six – The root focus of prayer from God's perspective is for you and me to depend on Him every time we pray and not so much for us to get answers.

## II. PRAYER ATTITUDE/METHODS/
## TIME MANAGEMENT

Day Seven – A prayer scope based on looking downwards and around is limited, but a prayer scope from above lets you soar like an eagle and remain balanced.

Day Eight – Harmonizing my prayer perspective with God's perspective through His Word has an extraordinary way of ensuring effectiveness in praying.

Day Nine – When we pray from a longing heart for God guided by His word, our prayers hit the target. When we pray selfishly, we pray amiss.

Day Ten – Praying haphazardly isn't okay. We should never allow the circumference of our prayers be determined by external factors.

Day Eleven – A maximized prayer time entails allowing your whole being to cooperate with the physical promptings of the Holy Spirit.

Day Twelve – Praying yourself into God's manifest presence while intentionally staying focused prepares you for precise prayers that yield results.

Day Thirteen – The place of prayer is not a physical location, although a physical location can help you quickly get into the manifest presence of the Lord.

Day Fourteen – Discipline cultivates quiet, heart-intense prayers. This art is particularly relevant to all growing and driven individuals.

Day Fifteen – Heaven responds to putting a premium on prayer time.

Day Sixteen – When we say we cannot pray like the Old Testament prophet Daniel, we forget that growth occurs in stages.

Day Seventeen – A high-powered rifle or any gun will ensure damage, even with a silencer. Whether you pray loudly or quietly, what matters is the heart intensity.

Day Eighteen – When praying for big personal life events, think in bite-size. You can easily muster the faith to face it in small chunks.

Day Nineteen – One wields influence through prayer because one makes the most of the time one has.

Day Twenty – Pray ahead of time to keep from straying in time. When you pray early, you get to hear clearly, and you don't pay dearly.

Day Twenty-one – Wisdom requires that we pray proactively and not reactively. Consistently praying reactively brings into question our spiritual growth.

Day Twenty-two – Prayer is valuable and measurable. Subjecting prayer to measurement removes ambiguity in our expectation and enhances its value.

Day Twenty-three – In an extended time of prayer, it is advisable to pace yourself and even have an outlined prayer point listing. The flow is not broken.

## III. PRAYER CONTENT

Day Twenty-four – Prayer is not rocket science, but there is an art form to the madness. All prayers revolve around engagements with our Heavenly Father, satanic forces, ourselves, and our environment.

Day Twenty-Five – Seasons of thanksgiving and year round thankful prayers help in releasing our prayer burdens to the Lord when we feel heavy hearted.

Day Twenty-Six – Christians gathering to worship and pray enhance Heaven and Earth's courtship, while Jesus gets the Lordship.

Day Twenty-Seven – Prayer is universal. Exposure to our global siblings praying to the Father helps broaden our prayer understanding. Take time to hear others.

Day Twenty-Eight – Intercede for government leaders that they may promote policies for peaceful daily living.

## IV. RESULTS

Day Twenty-Nine – God answering our prayers is not a sign that we prayed an effective prayer or that we are living godly lives.

Day Thirty – The greatest prayer legacy parents can give to our children is to pray that they become greater than us in their generation.

www.ingramcontent.com/pod-product-compliance
Lightning Source LLC
Chambersburg PA
CBHW071420040426
42445CB00012BA/1230